The Blueprint to revive Indian Economy

Prologue: India has 1.3 Billion People. Indians are most hardworking and talented, yet engineers in India cannot get even a Rupees 11000 job and MBA graduates in India fight for Rupees 5000 job. Delhi –the capital of India is one of the filthiest place of world, Mumbai has stink of sewer everywhere. Whereas a Biryani shop owner in Hyderabad –MD Shakeel drives in his Honda City and lives a joyful life in his posh bungalow. This book analyzes the gap and provides solution to problems in India.

Chapters

1. The traditional economy versus the new economy
2. Main Problem Areas
3. Changing the Education System
4. Pain Points could be the gain Points
5. Renewable Energy
6. Roads
7. Transportation
8. Agriculture and Allied Industries
9. Internet and Virtual Currency
10. Food
11. Courts and Jails
12. Promoting Entrepreneurship
13. Working Abroad

14. Foreigners Working in India
15. Healthcare
16. ITES and BPO
17. Small Self-Help Groups
18. Tourism
19. Fun and Frolic

Please follow us on Twitter @rajmehatalb

And Subscribe to our YouTube Channel:
https://www.youtube.com/channel/UCxd4UCONGTM63ii4edmK1rA

Visit us at: www.kalkie.org, www.igurucool.in, www.kalkie.in for more books

Explore working with us at: http://www.igurucool.in/earn.html

Chapter One: The Traditional Economy versus New Economy

I am neo-liberal, I work as ladies supervisor. I do online shopping and even eat masala dosa on the street. I am sixty years old and have seen India through the eyes of my kids, grand-children and my own. I am strong advocate of the fact that if engineering and mba colleges do not make our kids earn the education expense in first three years, then they should return the student the deficit amount. In education loan, the institutes should also be made debtor, and within three years if student does not repay the loan amount, the fees should be extracted from the institute. From 2020 onwards, it should be made mandatory by government that all children obtain his/her engineering, medical or mba degree on education loan and if child is unable to repay loan –the fault is with the institute and they should pay the education dues.

I had a very funny incident today. My friend Jitu used to bring cigarettes for me. Since past few years, the price of cigarette has been increasing and my budget used to get disturbed. Seeing the family condition, I curtailed on one pack of cigarette and started smoking weed in the gap. My daily expense came down from Rupees 200 to Rupees 120, and I started saving Rupees 2400 per month for my three kids.

I noticed that price of pure desi cigarette pack was Rupees 35, and Jitu was charging Rupees 50 per pack from me. I negotiated it to Rupees 90 for two packs and started saving Rupees 300 per month additionally.

The benefit of Modi Government at Centre is that many desi companies have started grooming, and I get the same product at much lower price.

Initially there was stranglehold of ITC on tobacco, but now I see that ITC has almost vanished from the shops. There are many new companies and making good money.

**

I have some petty work from home options for poor and middle class readers, who can earn $20 per month from home. Please join these options at: http://www.igurucool.in/earn.html

Another option for you to earn is ChampCash which is available at Google Play Store for Android Phones. Join ChampCash with Sponsor Id

(Mandatory): 11233739 and earn few hundred extra bucks per month by shopping, seeing ads, filling surveys and referring others.

**

India is a Rich Country if total assets are taken into consideration, but poor country if per capita income is calculated. By this analogy top 5 Rich Countries of World are: China, India, USA, Russia and Brazil. But real wealth is reflected only in USA –with high standard of living.

$60000 Per Annum is below median salary in USA, but in India if someone gets $60000 he can spend whole life without doing anything and feeding on interest from fixed deposit in bank or post-office.

**

The ideal income for an average Indian is Rupees 25000 per month. If he has Rupees 41 Lakhs in fixed deposit then it will yield Rupees 23500 as bank interest and another Rupees 1500 per month, he can earn from internet.

But for poor people of India Rupees 6100 per month is sufficient, and I am living in Utopia that by magic wand the target of Rupees 25000 and Rupees 6100 would be met.

**

Now let me breakup the expense of an average Indian, who is able to earn Rupees 25000 per month.

- House Rent – Rs 6000
- Food –Rs 8000
- Education of Two Kids – Rs 8000

- Miscellaneous –Rs 3000

Now let me break up expense of a poor Indian, who may get Rupees 6100 per month.

- House –Rs 1500
- Food –Rs 2000
- Education of 2 Kids –Rs 1500
- Miscellaneous –Rs 1100

So in an ideal situation we should get this money. This is bare necessity for our survival.

**

Please follow us on Twitter @rajmehatalb

And Subscribe to our YouTube Channel: https://www.youtube.com/channel/UCxd4UCONGTM63ii4edmK1rA

**

The traditional economy of India consisted of shops, jewelers, ironsmith, carpenter and vegetable sellers. There were few inns and eating joints. India had few sweet-seller shops.

There were two phases in the modernization of Indian Economy: First when there was nationalization of banks and second in 1991 –when Manmohan Singh started globalization of India.

The new economy consists of IT companies, BPOs, Consultancy firms, Private Banks and Mobile Companies. But only 2% of Indians got employment in the torch-bearers of new economy. Remaining 98% of

Indians are in dilemma – to start something of their own in old economy or become a feeder to new economy.

**

Chapter Two: Main Problem Areas

The main problem areas of Indian Economy are identified below:

- Lack of enough enterprise to employ everybody
- Rude behavior of employers
- Lack of funding opportunities
- Lack of skills
- High enterprise cost
- Competition from foreign companies
- Lack of good ideas
- Lethargy of employees
- Illiteracy
- Lack of micro enterprises
- No bank accounts
- Poor vision of leaders
- Poor infrastructure
- Low return on investment

**

Chapter Three: Changing the Education System

I have two wives and three kids. My first wife is a famous model and lives in South Africa along with my seventeen year old boy. She handles my brother's entire business and lives in a lavish $40 Million Rand house, which has pools, barbeque, fire place and attic. I never visit her, but she visits me when I come to Delhi. This time when I visited Delhi, there was severe cash crisis and she spent Rupees 5, 61,000 on her credit card to buy fashionable dressed for my in-laws and few dresses and electronics goods for my two daughters.

My son Roy is very sharp and initially wanted to become Pilot. But now he wants to become a Movie Star in Hollywood. For that reason my wife would be moving to Hollywood within three-four years. She is a good writer, dress-designer, good interior designer and a fabulous cook.

On an average she makes $6 Million per year and she is fiercely protective about her son, so she stays away from me. She fears that I would put my son in Indian education system and like me he would end up earning Rupees 20,000 per month.

But my daughters are strict adherer of Indian Education System and all they want to compete in IIT –not knowing what happens after engineering in India.

Now let me tell you about myths and folklores in India. Every kid thinks either of becoming Engineer, Doctor or IAS in India. Now 80% of engineers in India are unemployed, doctors are doing well at median salary of Rs 31000 per month and in UPSC only 438 candidates get selected out of 4 lakh odd candidates appearing every year,

Not a single kid talks in India about opening his own business, whereas in USA 13 year old kids start earning by selling soda pops, crush candy and doing car wash. If India has to change then right from age of 13 or 14 the kids should be taught about earning money.

I made my first income of Rupees 15 at age of 11 by selling datoons (neem sticks) and Rupees 65 at the age of 15, by opening a comics library. My best friend Sanjay Surana was my avid customer, and from there I learnt how to value and respect every single customer.

You get immense pleasure when a customer pays you and gives you a positive feedback. If a child gets this feeling at young age, his spirit would change once and forever.

**

Chapter Four: Pain Points could be Gain Points

My love story would tell you –how pain points could be gain points. When I was studying in an Engineering College in West Bengal, I used to chat for hours with American Friends on Linux Systems. There used to be chat rooms and chatting was addiction for almost everybody in college.

I befriended an ordinary looking girl called Kavita Ram in Singapore and she called me there in either July or August 1998 (I do not exactly remember) for Shahrukh Khan Concert. She paid for everything, but on reaching Singapore I returned all her money, because my payment for a USA based project was credited by time. That was the first and last flight of my life because our flight was caused in turbulence in stormy weather, and all of us in flight had near death experience in the plane. (I returned to India on cruise).

Well in the Shahrukh Khan concert, there were many Russian, Chinese and South African models who were giving performance. Till that time I had never seen blondes and my eye was fixated on a particular South

African Model. I shared this with Kavita and she immediately introduced me to her, and in return I gave Kavita a slam book personally signed by King himself. Kavita was happy with Shah Rukh Khan Autograph and I was very happy to be with Natty.

I asked Natty —"How much do you earn?"

She replied "$105 per show."

I said —"I will make you rich if you agree to become my girlfriend."

She gladly agreed and we stayed for a week in Oberoi hotel —where Kavita's father was chief executive chef.

I and Natty worked out a detailed business plan, where she used her beauty to become one of the highest paid celebrities in South Africa, and I stopped working on foreign projects, because Natty used to send me huge amount of money.

We had a kid in August 1999 and we married in January 2001 in Mumbai. After our marriage we rarely met, but now she has assets more than $100 Million USD.

The simple trick which I taught her —"Script your own Success". She wrote movie scripts like Sylvester Stallone on her own. She wrote her Talk Show script on her own, and had a very popular YouTube Channel.

The journey from $100 a show to $100 Million was long, but from being a cheerleader to celebrity was a short journey. She became celebrity as early as June 2002.

**

So India has some negative areas like sanitation, housing, electricity, roads, railways etc. So these are the areas where mass can be pushed into and almost everybody could (at least) get a part-time job. Our government should identify India's weaknesses and put our manpower in these areas.

**

This is true because in Bollywood 95% of films flop due to poor script, and if in Stallone style actors start writing their own script, their films would be massive grosser.

**

Natty does not stay with me because of two reasons –the linguistic barrier and behavior of my father. Natty does not understand a word in Hindi and my Parents do not understand her language. Secondly Natty was shocked at the behavior of my father, when I introduced her to him. He all of sudden started abusing her without any reason.

**

So it depends upon the Government to find suitable people who would fit in a particular industry. If we put misfits then Vision 2020 would be ruined.

**

Chapter Five: Renewable Energy

India has one of the largest coal reserves in World, but due to logistics there are severe power-cuts. Renewable energy is answer to it. The process for renewable energy is:

- Installation of independent solar cell in each house
- Creating large wind farms in southern and western India
- Making large solar plants to the capacity of 4200 MW in every state and connecting it to national electricity grid
- Making Biodiesel through Jathropa and use it in scaling up fuels in Industry.

**

Chapter Six: Roads

Few days back I was going to RIMS hospital in Ranchi. In order to save money, the autorickshawallah took me through the streets of Ranchi, and then I felt how bad the roads of India were. Just by building Highways, the road crisis could not be solved. You have to build roads in village and in the streets of towns. The five point agenda to solve the road crisis of India is:

- Connect every village in India with at least 6 meter road
- Broaden old, narrow roads to at least 6 meter through MNREGA
- Pass law for autorickshaw owners and taxi drivers that they would be fined Rs 1000 if caught driving on narrow roads to earn extra money.
- Build an alternate National Highway parallel to existing national highways
- Stop decongestion in Big Cities by building parallel roads.

**

Chapter Seven: Transportation

India has good transportation facilities but it lacks depth. There are rickshawallah doing manual labour, there are autorickshaw which are unsafe. The buses are hot and uncomfortable. There is low penetration of services like UBER and Ola. The #eleven point #agenda to revamp the transportation is:

- Inventing new safe and sturdy autorickshaw and phasing out rickshaw
- Giving new rickshaw to rickshawallah at 2% interest rate
- Building Transport Nagar after every 5 kilometer in town/city for rickshaw and cab owners
- Starting a new transport company on PPP model and phasing out old buses
- Starting SMS and APP based services with high penetration
- Insuring every passengers, irrespective of any mode of public transport they take.
- The insurance amount should be Rupees 11 Lakh
- Ensuring Digital Entertainment in every mode of public transport
- Ensuring Wireless Swipe Card in every public transport facility
- Enabling a PPP company, enlisting street vendors to supply food on Public Transport
- Building State Run Transport Training college for training Drivers and Mechanics.

**

Chapter Eight: Agriculture and Allied Industries

India is Krishi-Pradhan desh and 70% of population is involved in Agriculture directly or indirectly. Yet many people face problems.

The main problems faced are:

- Drought
- Lack of irrigation
- Lack of credit facility
- Crop Insurance
- Good price for crop
- Lack of cheap fertilizers
- All year round employment
- Machinery for cultivation

The solutions are:

- Large scale cultivation of cash crops like Jathropa which yields bio-diesel
- Constructing National water-grid to fight drought and flood
- Making water-pumps through PSUs and distributing them at subsidy
- Giving Farmers credit up to 200% of their last year income
- Ensuring every crop yield
- Make a national crop exchange which fixes the price of Agricultural Produce and do trading like Bitcoins
- Establishing giant PSUs which produce bulk fertilizers –organic and in-organic at cheap price.
- Employing Farmers all-round the year through MNREGA.
- Establishing high-tech farm equipment PSUs along with China, Russia, USA and Japan and make farming almost mechanical.

**

Chapter Nine: Internet and Virtual Currency

Internet has the power that people can work from home. Since 2009, I am at home and earning only through Internet. You can start a small venture and earn from Internet. The ideas are:

- Consultancy
- E commerce Site
- Service Provider
- Exchange

From last few years I have been earning BitCoins from Internet from faucets. The government has two options –either to adopt BitCoins or start a new digital currency, where people would be paid for doing small tasks.

To get a feel of earning from home visit
http://www.igurucool.in/earn.html

**

Chapter Ten: Food

Food is the basic necessity and everyone loves good food. There is severe scarcity of good eating joints in India. The contour has been changing since coming of Mc Donalds, Pizza Hut and Domino's but 82% (GARTNER RESEARCH) of Indians are still aching for tasty food.

The place where I live has no restaurants nearby, and I have either go 3 kilometer away in car, or to order food at home from vendors 3-5 kilometers away.

Now this is sector where government can do nothing because of scope and scale of operation. Here something can be done only by private companies.

The suggestions are:

- Opening of at least 23 Pan India Food Chains by private parties
- Home delivery to every nook and corner of India
- Having APP, SMS or Internet based service where food can be ordered at home.

Remember in India, alone, it is a $7 Trillion Industry (Gartner Research).

**

Chapter Eleven: Courts and Jails

In India, courts and jails are in shabby state. A lot of work is needed in them. Let us deal with the problems of courts first.

- There is no proper seating arrangement in court
- Court Records are kept in Paper –which is difficult to manage
- There is no seating arrangement in court complex for lawyers
- There is no urinal or lavatory in #hazaat
- The lawyers charge arbitrarily –which is bad for them and for client
- There is no strong room for court papers
- The toilets in court complex are dirty
- The lawyers sit in open, unprotected from Rain and Sun
- There is no proper food arrangement in court.

The solutions for these problems are:

- Building new court complex in phased manner, with modern sitting arrangement.
- Digitize court records, destroy paper confessions after six months
- 'Make modern seating arrangement in court for lawyers and clients
- Build modern #hazaats with proper seating, reclining facilities and toilets
- There should be fixed charge depending upon the maturity of case, highest first, lowest at last
- A digital complex something like #blockchain technology should be built for court records
- Make good and hygienic toilet complex in courts
- Make good rest-rooms for lawyers
- There should be proper food courts in courts.

**

There are only four reforms suggested for jails:

- Build modern jails with good sleeping facilities
- Give good food to inmates
- Build proper toilets
- Engage inmates into proper jobs, if nothing, then at least they can earn from Internet.

**

Chapter Twelve: Promoting Entrepreneurship

Entrepreneurs are backbone of any economy. More entrepreneurs' means more jobs in the society. The western world and China, Japan developed so much because of entrepreneurs. In India the startups fail because of reasons listed below:

- Engineers and MBA start most of their venture in Internet domain, which is cluttered and has high operational expense.
- They do not have access to cheap credit facility
- The visibility of entrepreneurs are poor
- The entrepreneurs think about making quick buck.
Please read our book "From Startup to IPO" on
http://www.igurucool.in/books.html

The solutions to entrepreneurial problems in India are:
- Having a venture capital fund of Rupees 10 Lakh Crore which gives out loan at 4% Annum
- To use internet as enabler, not the means. For example UBER is advertised on Internet and is App based, but the service is Physical
- To have boot camps in every college about startups
- Make students accessible to high quality Management Books
- Put the upper bar of Management colleges or B-school fees to Rupees 5 lakh for complete course; because whatever taught in management is shit and students find it difficult to get even a Rupees 5000 job.
- Open "Subhash Employment Guarantee Scheme (SEGS) center all across India.
http://www.slideshare.net/RajatMehta46/blueprint-of-mission-segs-subhash-employment-guarantee-scheme
Or
https://www.youtube.com/watch?v=e66psF9uR_4

**

Chapter Thirteen: Working Abroad

It is a global economy and some Indians work abroad. This is good for country as it brings foreign exchange; but the problem arises when eight Indians are locked in a small room, their passport is snatched and they have to starve for days. So there are some basic rules for Indians working abroad:

- Their minimum monthly salary should be $6000.
- They get well-furnished Accommodation
- They get on-campus food
- They are allowed to spend 15 days in India in a year (mandatory) – just to check whether they are safe or not.

**

Chapter Fourteen: Foreigners Working in India

India has now become land of opportunity. People want to work in companies and join the spiritual mission. But India should be considerate while employing foreigners, because one dissatisfied person would turn away thousand others. Here are the rules:

- The foreigners should work only above managerial post –with minimum salary of $6000 per month.
- They should be provided furnished accommodation in good locality
- They should be given on-campus food.

- They should be given free-of-cost travel to places of tourist attraction and spirituality in India –twice a year.
- There should be three categories of countries A, B and C. People from A category countries should be given Visa-on-Arrival.

**

Chapter Fifteen: Healthcare

In India if you go to private hospital, they charge you exorbitant fees, if you go to government hospital they will make you stand in long queues. So there has to be middle path, and that comes through PPP model (Public Private Participation). The solutions are:

- Opening the autonomous PPP hospital country-wide with moderate fees.
- Opening a small hospital in every village.
- Opening Pharma companies in PPP model
- Regulate Private hospitals through Price bands and making it mandatory for them to have 20% patients BPL card holder with fees not more than 5000 Rupees per person in a year.
- Build more Government Hospitals.
- Opening a new line of Modern Ambulance Chain.

**

Chapter Sixteen: ITES and BPO

For last six years I had been trying to earn a dollar through freelancing sites like freelancer.com and upwork.com etc., but I did not earn a penny from them, instead I lost $156 in freelancer.com to a pig.

Whatever I have earned is from fiverr.com –which is #1 freelancing site in the world.

India has many tech-savvy IT enthusiasts who can make logo, design websites, do SEO and lot of other things.

The IT companies of India pick engineering graduates like bhend-bakri (sheep-goat) and make them work for Rupees 11000 per month for years. The good companies like Google, Facebook, Oracle, Adobe, and Cisco treat employees well, nurture them and give them good salary, but they employ less than 0.023% of engineering graduates.

In call centers, the atmosphere is much better than IT companies, because they do not have pressure to perform, but there salary is very low.

So remedies for ITES and BPO sectors are:

- Leave the BPO sector untouched as it is doing good and prospering
- Launch Government IT companies like Infosys –who would handle bulk foreign project
- Launch a freelancing site like upwork.com –the revenue potential is $42 Billion per year
- Launch a government payment gateway like payumoney.com which can also accept Bitcoins and transfer money to Indian Bank Accounts
- Under #skillindia launch IT training centers like NIIT, which trains one in software as well as hardware.

**

Chapter Seventeen: Small Self-Help Groups

There are tens of enterprises which can be started with capital as low as Rupees 1 Lakh. The broad plan is to collect 500 individuals and collect Rupees 10000 each from them and start 50 enterprises in which 10 people handle one enterprise. This is communist philosophy but it will be very successful.

The sectors in which this model can be successfully implemented are:

- Chicken Farming
- Eggs
- Shop
- Vegetable Farming
- Milk and Dairy
- Bread and Biscuit
- Mobile Recharge Shop
- Xerox Shop
- Utensil Shop
- Cloth Shop

**

Chapter Eighteen: Tourism

India is a tourism hot-spot, only its potential needs to be explored. To start with, we have to build six tourist circuits.

- Buddha Circuit – starting from Gaya to entire Orissa, West Bengal, Jharkhand and Bihar.

- Shiv Hari Circuit – It will consist of Varanasi, Haridwar and Rishikesh
- Goa Circuit – It will consist of Goa, Pune, Lonavala, Mumbai, Nagpur and Shirdi along with Shani Shingapur
- South Circuit – It will consist of Kerala, Tamilnadu, Andhra Pradesh, Karnataka and Andaman and Nicobar Islands
- Central Circuit – It will consist of Madhya Pradesh, Chattisgarh, Parts of Maharashtra and Rajasthan
- The North-East Circuit – Consisting Darjeeling and entire North-East States

Each circuit to have its own taste, cuisine and speciality.

The essential items for promoting tourism would be:

- Good Food
- Female Escorts
- Cheap Hotels
- Sale of Handicrafts
- Prayer Halls
- Spiritual Centers
- Medical Facilities
- Good Cabs
- ATMs
- Security
- Jewelry
- Ethnic Clothes
- Special Tourist Trains connecting circuits

**

Chapter Nineteen: Fun and Frolic

Fun and Frolic has very important role in the growth of economy. During my visit to Las Vegas, I found out how fast money changed hands. It is this sector of economy in which money moves @thespeedoflight.

The work needed to be done is:

- One Pub in each town
- One PVR style movie theatre in each town
- One Museum in each town
- One Zoological Park in each town
- One Amusement Park in each town

**

Epilogue: The purpose of writing this book is to reach entrepreneurs – who need guidance and invest in these sectors. Please contact us at: http://www.kalkie.org

**

End of Book

www.ingramcontent.com/pod-product-compliance
Lightning Source LLC
Chambersburg PA
CBHW041122180526
45172CB00001B/375